THE
STEAMER
COOKBOOK
LORNA RHODES

MARTIN BOOKS

Published by Martin Books
Simon & Schuster International Group
Fitzwilliam House 32 Trumpington Street
Cambridge CB2 1QY
in association with
Swan Housewares Ltd
Swan House Albion Street Birmingham B1 3DL

First published 1989
© Woodhead-Faulkner (Publishers) Ltd 1989
ISBN 0 85941 576 7 (hardback)
0 85941 577 5 (paperback)
Conditions of sale

Lorna Rhodes is an experienced cookery writer and
home economist who has worked for several major food
companies. She is now a freelance consultant, author
and contributor to numerous magazines, and a busy
working mother.

Design: Barry Lowenhoff
Photography: David Burch
Food preparation for photography: Lorna Rhodes
Author's photograph: David Boni
Typesetting: Goodfellow & Egan Ltd, Cambridge
Printed and bound in Great Britain by
The Eagle Press plc, Blantyre

The publishers would like to thank Wendy Veale
for her help with this book.

The publishers gratefully acknowledge David Mellor Ltd
for cutlery and Wedgewood Ltd for crockery used in
photographs in this book.

Contents

INTRODUCTION

Steaming as a method of cooking has been used for many thousands of years, especially in the East: since ancient times, sophisticated oriental cuisine has featured steaming. Steaming is a quick, healthy and natural way of cooking to retain flavour and nutrients, which makes it perfect for today's lifestyles.

Steaming is often associated with heavy, stodgy puddings, or fish that is bland in flavour and colour. This collection of recipes will quickly dispel any such ideas, as the dishes have been developed for healthy eating, using fresh ingredients. Steaming retains the natural colour, flavour and nutritional value of the food, and it is also gentle enough to ensure that the texture and shape of delicate ingredients are not lost.

Steaming is extremely versatile: there are many different foods which can be steamed to produce exciting dishes, for everyday family meals as well as sophisticated dinner parties. Steaming is also ideal for cooking meals for vegetarian, slimming and other specialist diets, as well as for generally healthy food. In addition the recipes have no extra calories added, the cholesterol level is kept low, the sauces are carefully prepared using the cooking juices collected from the foods and wherever possible high-fat ingredients have been omitted.

ADVANTAGES OF THE SWAN STEAM COOKER

The Steam Cooker makes it possible to cook a whole meal at once, without transferring the flavours of the different foods to each other. This can give savings of up to 30 per cent in time and fuel compared to more conventional cooking methods.

One of the delights of the Steam Cooker is the freedom it gives you. A 120-minute timer means that there is no need to check food constantly during cooking, and no matter where food is placed in the Steam Cooker it will cook perfectly. There is no chance of burning or sticking, and no need to baste or turn food over.

The Steam Cooker is thermostatically controlled to ensure that it is always at the correct temperature.

The transparent lid enables you to see at a glance how cooking is progressing; when food needs attention take off the lid (turning it away from the face) and lift out the tray or basket away from the steam.

The drip collection tray ensures that no valuable juices are lost, and these can be used as a basis for stocks, soups and sauces.

Components of the Swan Steam Cooker

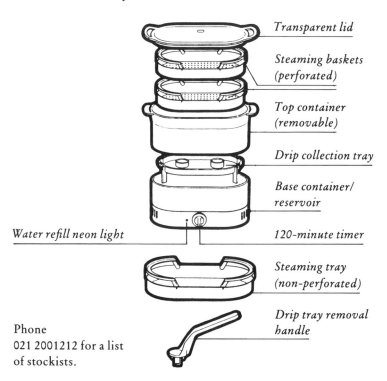

Transparent lid

Steaming baskets
(perforated)

Top container
(removable)

Drip collection tray

Base container/
reservoir

Water refill neon light

120-minute timer

Steaming tray
(non-perforated)

Drip tray removal
handle

Phone
021 2001212 for a list
of stockists.

THE BENEFITS OF STEAMING

Steaming is a moist heat cooking method, which means that added fat can be kept to a minimum – ideal for slimmers as well as for a generally healthy diet.

Steaming preserves the natural goodness and flavour of food, which means that added salt can be kept to a minimum or cut out completely. Try using other seasonings and fresh herbs, and add only a little salt, if necessary, at the end of the cooking process.

The steamer can be used to reheat food – heat penetrates through the food gently so there is no risk of the food drying up.

The steamer can be used to keep food warm, which is especially useful when entertaining. It is best to place the food in a suitable container; then cover with foil and stand in a basket in the steamer.

The steamer can be used to skin tomatoes and fruit. Place the fruit in a basket and steam for 3–4 minutes; then plunge into cold water. The skin will then peel away easily. Almonds, too, can be peeled in this way.

The steamer is the ideal companion to the freezer: use it for blanching vegetables and fruit prior to freezing. Blanching is simple: just place the prepared fruit or vegetables in a basket and steam for 3–8 minutes, depending on the size, shape and density of the food. Plunge into cold water and the food is then ready for freezing.

The steamer can also be used for defrosting, since the steam penetrates the food evenly from all directions. For best results, wrap the food in a piece of foil and place in the preheated steamer. A 1.5 kg (3 lb) chicken can be defrosted in 45–60 minutes.

USEFUL INFORMATION ABOUT COOKING IN THE STEAMER

To ensure maximum flavour use fresh stock when needed, but substitute stock cubes or water for stock if time is short.

The flavour of food can be enhanced by adding stock, wine, herbs, vegetables or flavourings to the cooking liquid in the reservoir.

When using the juices in the drip tray or the stock in the reservoir for the preparation of sauces, remove the stock from the reservoir and refill the reservoir with water before reheating. Transfer the food to a serving dish, cover with foil and return to the steamer to keep warm until the sauce is ready.

To prevent the possibility of fish sticking to baskets, lightly grease the baskets with butter before use.

Do not overfill the baskets and trays. As a general guide they should be no more than two-thirds full.

Check the level of liquid in the reservoir occasionally and add more water if the level is at or below the minimum marker, i.e. 🌙.

Always place the non-perforated tray above the basket when using them together, unless otherwise stated.

SUITABLE CONTAINERS TO USE IN THE STEAMER

Ovenproof glass or ceramic dishes,
Metal trays or containers,
Foil bowls or containers,
Folded pieces of foil,
Thick plastic containers, e.g. microwave quality,
Heatproof china dishes.

RECIPE NOTES

Ingredients are given in both metric and imperial quantities. Use either set of quantities, but not a mixture of both, in any one recipe.

All spoon measurements are level unless otherwise stated.

1 tablespoon = one 15 ml spoon; 1 teaspoon = one 5 ml spoon.

Eggs are standard (size three) unless otherwise stated.

All recipes use a basket unless otherwise stated.

All times given in charts and recipes are approximate cooking times and do not include the preheating time of the steamer.

The amount of water to use in the reservoir is marked as one of the three following litre quantities: ½ 1 1½. Approximate conversions are: 1 pint; 1¾ pints; 2½ pints. Other liquids and flavourings used in the reservoir are listed in the recipe ingredients.

STEAMING MEATS AND FISH
RED MEATS

For best results ensure steaks, chops, etc. are equally shaped and sized; this ensures even cooking. Joints should not be greater than 15 cm (6 inches) in diameter or less than 10 cm (4 inches). Steaks and chops should not be greater than 4 cm (1¾ inches) thick.

The 'cut' of meat also affects the cooking time – for best results use lean meat. Less tender joints should be cubed and cooked in stock in the non-perforated tray in the steamer.

Joints do not dry out with this method of cooking – there will be less shrinkage than when conventionally roasted. To 'enrich' the colour place them in a hot oven for a few minutes, just to colour the outside.

JOINTS			
Diameter	Approximate cooking time per pound (minutes)		
	'rare'	'medium'	'well done'
10–12 cm (4–4½ inches)	15	20	25
13–16 cm (5–6½ inches)	18–20	22–25	28–30

The 'rare' and 'medium' cooking times apply only for beef. For pork, lamb and other red meats follow cooking times given for 'well done'.

The Steamer Cookbook

STEAKS

Thickness	'rare'	'medium'	Cooking time (minutes) 'well done'
1–2 cm (½–¾ inch)	6–8	8–10	10–15
3 cm (1¼ inches)	10–14	15–18	18–22
4 cm (1½ inches)	14–18	18–20	22–25

WHITE MEATS, e.g. VEAL, POULTRY

Veal is a delicate textured meat and when cooked conventionally has a tendency to dry out easily; the steamer provides an ideal cooking method for this and other white meats.

VEAL

Cut	Weight	Cooking time (minutes)
Cutlets	175 g (6 oz)	15–20
Escalopes	175 g (6 oz)	18–20
Shoulder	1.05 kg (2¼ lb)	50–60

POULTRY

	Weight	Cooking time (minutes)
Whole birds	1.05 kg (2¼ lb)	60
Wings/legs	250 g (8 oz)	30–35
Breast	250 g (8 oz)	20–25

FISH

Steaming fish is the best way – the fish is cooked without sticking or disintegrating and the flesh is moist and tender. Whole fish gain in flavour if stuffed with herbs or lemon wedges before cooking. Freshwater fish require more seasoning than saltwater fish.

Fish	Cooking time (minutes)
Crustaceans, e.g. prawns	10–20
Mussels	5–8
Other molluscs, e.g. scallops	5–10
Whole fish	15–20
Small fish, fillets	10–15

STEAMING VEGETABLES AND FRUIT

Cut vegetables into small even-sized pieces for quick, even cooking. Vegetables can be cooked directly in baskets or wrapped in aluminium foil.

If vegetables to be cooked in the same basket include strongly coloured roots, such as carrots or beetroot, as well as others, such as potatoes or celery, it is advisable to separate them by strips of aluminium foil, folded to act as dividers so that the pale coloured vegetables do not become stained. The cooking times stated are to achieve *al dente* vegetables – the natural way with the vegetables still crisp.

VEGETABLES

	Maximum quantity per basket	Cooking time (minutes)	Preparation
Artichoke	3	45–60	Cut off stem close to base and remove outer dry or discoloured leaves. Soak in water for 15 minutes to clean. When cooked, leaves pull out easily.
Asparagus	375 g (12 oz)	10–15	Cut off woody ends and lightly scrape the white part with a knife towards tip.
Beans: French, Broad, Runner	375 g (12 oz)	25–30 (fresh) 20–25 (frozen)	Remove tops, tails and stringy sides. Slice large beans thickly, only small beans should be cooked whole.
Broccoli	375 g (12 oz)	20–25	Trim away thick, hard stalks.
Beetroot	2–4 beetroots 375 g (12 oz)	20–40	Do not remove skin of beetroot before cooking. Trim stalks. Cool before slicing.
Brussels sprouts	500 g (1 lb)	15–20 (fresh) 15–18 (frozen)	Trim stalks and remove outer leaves.
Cabbage	250 g (8 oz)	10–15	Remove coarse, damaged outer leaves and remove central core and hard stalks. Cut into wedges or break off leaves.
Cauliflower	1	20–25	Break into florets. Cook stem end down.
Carrots	375 g (12 oz)	25–35 (whole) 15–18 (sliced, diced) 10–15 (strips) 25–30 (frozen)	New carrots: scrub or scrape before cooking whole, or slice, cube or cut into strips. Old carrots: peel and slice, cube or cut into strips.
Celery	375 g (12 oz)	15–20	Cut off leaves before cooking. Break into sticks.
Courgettes	500 g (1 lb)	15–25 (whole) 10–15 (sliced)	Cut off ends but do not peel.
Corn on the cob	4	25–30 (fresh) 20–30 (frozen)	Trim off leaves and remove silky threads.
Leeks	500 g (1 lb)	20–30 (whole)	Remove coarse outer leaves, trim

9

		15–18 (sliced)	tops and roots. Split down centre to within 5 cm (2 inches) of root and wash thoroughly.
Marrow	1	15–20	Peel and cut in half lengthways. Remove seeds and cut into large cubes. Alternatively peel and cut into large rings, scooping out seeds from centre of each ring.
Parsnip	500 g (1 lb)	30–35	Remove stalk and root and peel thinly. Cut into quarters; then cut out core.
Peas	500 g (1 lb)	15–18 (fresh) 12–15 (frozen)	Remove from pods and wash before cooking. Pods can also be cooked and served as a vegetable.
Peppers	375 g (12 oz)	6–10 (sliced) 25–30 (whole)	Cut off stalk and remove inner seeds and white membrane. Cut into thick rings. Stuff whole peppers with crumpled aluminium foil before steaming to maintain shape.
Potatoes	375 g (12 oz)	30–35 (whole) 15–20 (sliced or cubed)	New potatoes: scrape or scrub skins, cook whole if small. Old potatoes: peel and slice or cube.
Spinach	250 g (8 oz)	5–10	Remove stalks before cooking.
Swede	500 g (1 lb)	20–35	Peel thickly and cut into chunks.
Turnip	500 g (1 lb)	20–35	Remove stalks and root and peel thinly. Cut into quarters; then slice or cube.
Fruit Apples	3 large	15–25	Core apples and score skin around middle.
Pears	4	25–35	Remove core from base, leave stalk and peel thinly.

STEAMING RICE AND PASTA

Rice can be cooked in the steamer and left to keep warm without the risk of drying out.
Part cook the rice for 5 minutes in boiling water; then spread over baskets in a shallow layer in the preheated steamer. With the cover in position, place a damp, cold cloth over the cover and steam for 15–20 minutes until soft.
When cooked, remove the baskets from the steamer and rinse the rice under running water for a few moments.
Fresh pasta can be cooked by the same method as rice. Lightly grease the baskets before laying out the pasta to prevent sticking.

Pasta shape	Cooking time (minutes)
Noodles	5 minutes boiling, 6–10 minutes steaming
Ravioli	5 minutes boiling, 12–15 minutes steaming
Cannelloni	5 minutes boiling, 12–15 minutes steaming

STEAMING EGGS AND EGG DISHES

Eggs can be cooked in several ways in the steamer, benefiting from the gentle cooking.

BOILED EGGS

Place the eggs directly in a basket in the preheated steamer and cook to the desired state: soft-boiled 7–8 minutes, hard-boiled 10–12 minutes.

POACHED

Lightly grease small basins, moulds or tea cups and fill to a third of their depth with water. Place in the preheated steamer and heat for 5 minutes. Place an egg in each container and cook for 6–7 minutes or until set. Pour off the water and remove the egg from the container.

SCRAMBLED

Place lightly beaten eggs directly into a lightly greased non-perforated tray, add milk (1–2 tablespoons) and seasonings. Steam for 6–8 minutes in the preheated steamer, stirring the mixture once as it begins to set.

EGG DISHES

Many recipes for egg-based mixture, custards, puddings, etc. require cooking in a bain-marie; these delicate dishes can be cooked to perfection in the steamer.
Always cover the top of the dish with a lid of aluminium foil to prevent condensation dripping over the surface of the mixture.

STEAMING PUDDINGS

A 1-litre (2-pint) pudding basin is the largest size that can be used in the steamer. Always lightly grease the basin before filling to enable the pudding to be removed without sticking or breaking.
It is important to make a tight fitting lid for the basin, to prevent steam entering and making the top of the pudding soggy. To make the lid use aluminium foil sheets or a double thickness of greaseproof paper. Make a wide pleat in the centre of the lid to allow for the pudding to rise and secure firmly with string.
To line a pudding bowl with suet pastry:
Roll out two-thirds of the pastry to a 5 mm (¼- inch) thickness. Fold gently into 4 and place the centre fold (the corner with no outer edges of pastry) in the centre of the base of the basin. Gently unfold the pastry and ease into shape so it fits. Spoon in the filling (sweet or savoury). Roll out the remaining pastry into a circle to make the lid. Dampen the edges of the pastry lining the basin. Place the circle on top and press the edges together firmly. Trim off any excess pastry.

Type of pudding	Cooking time (hours)
Suet (1-litre/1¾- pint basin)	2–3
Sponge (900 ml/1½-pint basin)	1–1¼
Christmas pudding (900 ml/1½-pint basin)	4–6 (plus reheating time)

FISH AND SHELLFISH DISHES

Korma Fish Kebabs

SERVES 4

Serve with a tomato and onion salad and poppadums.

500 g (1 lb) skinned
monkfish fillets
6 Mediterranean
prawns, shelled
16 mussels
12 pineapple cubes

MARINADE

6 tablespoons natural
yogurt
1 tablespoon oil
1 tablespoon mild
curry powder
1 garlic clove, crushed
½ teaspoon Tabasco
sauce
grated rind and juice
of 1 lime

GARNISH

1 lime, sliced or cut
into wedges
fresh coriander leaves

🥄 Put the ingredients for the marinade into a bowl and mix.

Cut the monkfish into cubes and cut the prawns in half; then fold into the marinade with the mussels. Cover and chill for 4–6 hours.

Thread the fish and pineapple on to 8 small bamboo skewers and lay them in the non-perforated tray; spoon over the marinade. Steam for 5–8 minutes or until the fish is firm and white.

Serve on a bed of rice, garnished with lime and coriander.

Korma Fish Kebabs

Coquilles St Jacques
SERVES 4

500 g (1 lb) scallops
*1 teaspoon lemon
    juice*
*125 ml (4 fl oz) dry
    white wine*
1 bay leaf
25 g (1 oz) butter
40 g (1½ oz) flour
*150 ml (5 fl oz) single
    cream*
*a pinch of Cayenne
    pepper*
*50 g (2 oz) Gruyère
    cheese, grated*
*500 g (1 lb) potatoes,
    boiled and
    creamed*
salt and pepper
*sprigs of fresh
    flat-leafed parsley,
    to garnish*

🌶 Wash the scallops and put into a basket.
Sprinkle over the lemon juice, and cook for
5 minutes until they are just tender. Lift the
scallops out of the steamer and cut the body
parts in half, leaving the orange corals whole.
Set them aside.

Pour the juices in the drip tray into a
saucepan, add the wine, bay leaf and a pinch of
salt, and simmer for 3 minutes; then strain into
a jug.

Melt the butter in the saucepan, stir in
the flour, and then gradually add the liquid in
the jug; return to the heat. Stir the sauce
continuously and bring to the boil, simmering
for 2 minutes. Stir in the cream, Cayenne
pepper and half the cheese and cook until the
cheese melts. Fold in the scallops and season if
necessary. Cook gently for 2 minutes.

Pipe a border of mashed potato around
the edges of 4 scallop shells or dishes, spoon
the scallops into the centre, and sprinkle with
the remaining cheese. Place under a hot grill
for 3–4 minutes until golden. Serve garnished
with parsley.

FISH AND SHELLFISH DISHES

Haddock Terrine

SERVES 6

This terrine can be served hot or cold; it makes an elegant party dish.

butter for greasing
750 g (1½ lb) smoked haddock fillets, skinned
150 ml (¼ pint) soured cream
2 eggs, separated
a good pinch of grated nutmeg
½ teaspoon ground turmeric
375 g (12 oz) fresh haddock fillets, skinned
grated rind of ½ lemon
3 teaspoons lemon juice
1 tablespoon chopped fresh parsley
salt and pepper

SAUCE
4 tablespoons mayonnaise
6 tablespoons natural yogurt
½ cucumber
4 spring onions

GARNISH
125 g (4 oz) whole prawns
sprigs of fresh dill

❶ Line the base of a 1 kg (2 lb) loaf tin with greaseproof paper and butter the base and sides.

Put the smoked haddock into a food processor and work to a purée. Transfer to a bowl and fold in the cream, egg yolks, nutmeg and turmeric. Whisk the egg whites until almost stiff; then fold into the fish mixture, and spoon half into the loaf tin.

Cut the fresh haddock into small pieces, discarding any bones, and mix with the lemon rind and juice and parsley; season lightly with salt and pepper. Spoon into the tin; then cover with the rest of the smoked haddock mixture. Cover with foil, place in a basket and steam for 40 minutes.

Meanwhile make the sauce. Mix together the mayonnaise and yogurt. Peel and de-seed the cucumber and cut it into small cubes; chop the spring onions finely. Add them to the sauce and mix well.

To serve the terrine, invert on to a serving plate and peel off the paper. Garnish with prawns and sprigs of dill. Serve accompanied by the sauce.

15

Clockwise from top left:
Moules Marinière
Coquilles St Jacques
Haddock Terrine
Salmon and Prawn
Quenelles

Salmon and Prawn Quenelles

SERVES 4 AS A MAIN COURSE OR 6 AS A STARTER

Light and creamy, quenelles make an elegant dish served with lemon sauce.

500 g (1 lb) salmon tail, boned and skinned
125 g (4 oz) peeled prawns
1 tablespoon lemon juice
125 ml (4 fl oz) double cream
1 egg plus 1 egg white
salt and pepper
SAUCE
150 ml (¼ pint) fish stock
a strip of lemon rind
1 egg yolk
2 tablespoons double cream
GARNISH
sprigs of fresh chervil

🥄 Cut up the salmon and put it into a food processor with the prawns; work until finely chopped. Season, add the lemon juice, cream, egg and egg white and blend again until the mixture is thick. Turn into a bowl and chill for 1 hour.

To make the sauce, put the stock and lemon rind into a saucepan and simmer for 10 minutes. Remove from the heat, and discard the lemon rind. Beat the egg yolk and cream together, whisk into the sauce and reheat very gently. Do not allow to boil.

To cook the fish quenelles, slide spoonfuls of the mixture into a basket lined with greaseproof paper. Place in the steamer and steam for 5 minutes until they are set and cooked through. Serve with the sauce, garnished with sprigs of chervil.

Moules Marinière
SERVES 4

1 kg (2 lb) fresh mussels
1 carrot, sliced
1 onion, sliced
1 celery stick, sliced
a bouquet garni
150 ml (¼ pint) dry white wine
600 ml (1 pint) water

Scrub and de-beard the mussels. Put the carrot, onion, celery and bouquet garni into the reservoir, with the wine and water.

Place the mussels in 2 baskets and place in the steamer. Use the drip tray to catch the juices. Cook for 5–7 minutes by which time the mussels should have opened; discard any which remain closed.

Pour the juices from the drip tray into a

25 g (1 oz) butter
1 garlic clove,
    chopped finely
25 g (1 oz) plain
    flour
1 tablespoon chopped
    fresh parsley
salt and pepper

jug and make up to 300 ml (½ pint) with the liquid from the reservoir.

Melt the butter in a saucepan, add the garlic and sauté for 1 minute. Stir in the flour and cook for 1 minute. Then gradually add the liquid from the jug, whisking over a moderate heat until thickened. Simmer for 2–3 minutes. Remove from the heat and stir in the parsley. Season with salt and pepper.

Turn the mussels into a warm deep dish or soup tureen and pour over the sauce.

Haddock with Herb Sauce
SERVES 4

1 shallot, chopped
750 ml (1¼ pints) fish
    stock
a bouquet garni
750 g (1½ lb)
    haddock fillets,
    skinned
250 ml (8 fl oz)
    natural yogurt
2 tablespoons chopped
    fresh parsley
1 teaspoon chopped
    fresh tarragon
1 teaspoon Pernod
salt and pepper

Put the shallot into the reservoir, and add the fish stock and the bouquet garni.

Cut the fish into 4 portions, place them in baskets and cook the fish in the steamer for 10 minutes. Strain the juices collected in the drip tray into a saucepan and add 6 tablespoons of the stock from the reservoir. Boil to reduce to 2 tablespoons of liquid; then add the yogurt, herbs and Pernod, season well and heat gently. Transfer the fish to warm serving plates and spoon over the sauce.

Soused Herring

SERVES 4

A marvellous way of cooking this inexpensive fish.

4 medium-size
herring, cleaned
and boned
300 ml (½ pint) dry
white wine
6 tablespoons white
wine vinegar
juice of 1 lemon
4 bay leaves
1 teaspoon pickling
spice
1 teaspoon salt
6 black peppercorns
2 blades of mace
1 medium-size onion,
sliced into rings

❶ Cut the herring in half lengthways to give 8 fillets. Roll each up with the skin on the outside and place in an ovenproof dish which fits into the steamer.

Put the wine, vinegar and lemon juice into a jug and then pour over the fish. Scatter over the rest of the ingredients; then cover with foil and place in a basket in the steamer. Cook for 30 minutes.

Remove from the steamer and, with a slotted spoon, transfer the fish to a serving dish. Strain the cooking juices over the fish, discarding the flavourings. Allow to cool before serving.

Plaice Swirls

SERVES 4

Ask your fishmonger to skin the fillets for this very attactive dish.

6 medium-size plaice
fillets, skinned
250 g (8 oz) pink
trout fillets,
skinned
1 tablespoon fromage
frais
2 teaspoons lemon
juice
salt and pepper
SAUCE
25 g (1 oz) butter

❷ Cut the plaice fillets in half lengthways; season and set aside.

Cut the trout into small pieces and put into the food processor, with the fromage frais and lemon juice; work until finely chopped. Put the plaice fillets skinned side up on the work surface and spread the trout filling over each. Roll up from the wide end and place each roll on its side in a basket. Cook for 5–6 minutes.

Meanwhile, make the sauce. Melt the butter in a saucepan, add the onion and cook

*1 small onion,
 chopped finely
125 ml (4 fl oz) dry
 white wine
2 firm tomatoes,
 skinned, de-seeded
 and diced
2 tablespoons double
 cream
salt and pepper*

until soft. Pour in the wine and simmer to reduce by half. Add the cooking juices from the drip tray, and keep the fish warm while simmering the sauce to reduce by half again. Add the diced tomatoes and cream to the sauce and reheat, seasoning if necessary.

Pour the sauce on to 4 warm serving plates and place the fish rolls on top. Serve at once.

Gefillte Fish

SERVES 4–6

A traditional Jewish dish, often served as a first course with horseradish relish, this can be eaten hot or cold.

*750 g (1½ lb) white
 fish fillets, skinned,
 e.g. haddock and
 cod
1 small onion,
 chopped finely
1 tablespoon chopped
 fresh parsley
50 g (2 oz) ground
 almonds
2 tablespoons lemon
 juice
1 egg, beaten
2 tablespoons fresh
 breadcrumbs
salt and pepper
1 small carrot, sliced
 thinly, to garnish*

❶ Put the fish into a food processor and chop finely, or pass through a mincer. In a bowl combine the fish with the rest of the ingredients.

With wet hands form the mixture into balls, putting a slice of carrot on each. Place in baskets and steam for 20 minutes.

Oriental Cod Steaks
SERVES 4
A delicious way of cooking fish, especially good if needing a low-calorie meal.

4 cod steaks weighing
about 250 g (8 oz)
each
4 teaspoons sesame oil
4 spring onions,
shredded
2 teaspoons shredded
fresh root ginger
1 garlic clove,
chopped finely
8 teaspoons light soy
sauce
sesame seeds, toasted

🐟 Place each cod steak on a piece of greaseproof paper. Drizzle over the sesame oil and then divide the spring onions, ginger and garlic between them. Spoon over the soy sauce and then wrap the fish in the paper. Place in baskets inside the steamer and cook for 10–12 minutes.

Carefully unwrap the fish, transfer to warmed plates and spoon over a little of the cooking juice in the paper. Sprinkle the sesame seeds over the fish and serve.

Red Mullet 'en Papillotes'
SERVES 4

4 red mullet weighing
175–250 g (6–8 oz)
each, cleaned
3 tablespoons dry
vermouth
½ teaspoon fennel
seeds
25 g (1 oz) butter,
melted
4 sprigs of fresh dill
salt and pepper
SAUCE
2 tablespoons olive oil
1 small onion,
chopped
1 garlic clove, crushed

🐟 Place each fish on a piece of foil, and season the fish with salt and pepper. Pour over the vermouth, scatter the fennel seeds and spoon over the butter. Lay a sprig of dill on each fish and then wrap up the foil to make a parcel. Set this aside while making the sauce.

Put the oil into a saucepan, add the onion, garlic and peppers and cook slowly for about 10 minutes until soft. Add the stock and simmer for 15 minutes. Rub the sauce through a sieve and then season the purée.

Put the parcels of fish into a basket, place in the steamer and cook for about 10 minutes. Unwrap the fish and put on to warm serving plates to keep warm. Strain the fish juices from the foil into the red pepper

2 red peppers,
    de-seeded and
    chopped
150 ml (¼ pint)
    vegetable stock
salt and pepper
GARNISH
sprigs of fresh dill

sauce and reheat; pour over the fish and serve garnished with fresh dill.

Sole and Asparagus Rolls
SERVES 4

600 ml (1 pint) fish
    stock
150 ml (¼ pint) dry
    white wine
1 shallot, chopped
    finely
a bouquet garni
500 g (1 lb) asparagus
8 medium-size sole
    fillets, skinned
2 tablespoons chopped
    fresh dill or
    2 teaspoons dried
    dill
4 ripe tomatoes,
    skinned and
    chopped
1 teaspoon tomato
    purée
salt and pepper
chopped fresh dill,
    to garnish

Pour the stock and wine into the reservoir, adding the shallot and bouquet garni. Trim the asparagus, put into a basket and steam for 10 minutes.

Lay the sole fillets flat, skinned side up, season and sprinkle with half the dill. Divide the asparagus between them, and then roll up from the wide end. Place in the steamer in 2 baskets and steam for 15 minutes. Keep warm while making the sauce.

Pour the juices from the drip tray into a saucepan and add 150 ml (¼ pint) of the stock from the reservoir; simmer until reduced to about 150 ml (¼ pint). Add the tomatoes and tomato purée and season; simmer again for 5 minutes. Press through a sieve, return to the pan, stir in the rest of the dill and reheat.

Transfer the fish to a warm serving dish and pour the sauce around the rolls. Garnish with fresh dill.

Clockwise from top:
Red Mullet 'en
Papillotes'
Tarragon Salmon
Steaks
Sole and Asparagus
Rolls

Tarragon Salmon Steaks

SERVES 4

These salmon steaks can be served hot, but the flavour when cold is superb.

4 salmon steaks
  weighing 250 g
  (8 oz) each
4 tablespoons dry
  white wine
4 sprigs of fresh
  tarragon
salt and pepper

SAUCE

4 tablespoons
  mayonnaise
2 tablespoons single
  cream
1 teaspoon tarragon
  vinegar
1 teaspoon tomato
  purée

GARNISH

sprigs of fresh
  tarragon
lemon wedges

🕐 Place each salmon steak on a piece of greaseproof paper large enough to wrap it up, season and then pour over the wine. Lay a sprig of tarragon on each steak; then wrap the fish in the paper and place in the steamer. Cook for 10 minutes. Allow to cool and chill until needed.

To make the sauce, put all the ingredients into a bowl and whisk together.

To serve, unwrap the fish, adding any juices to the sauce. Discard the tarragon and remove the skin from each steak, if wished. Place on serving plates and spoon some of the sauce over, garnishing with fresh sprigs of tarragon and lemon wedges. Any extra sauce can be served separately.

MEAT DISHES

Veal Rolls Marsala
SERVES 4

500 g (1 lb) veal
    escalopes
175 g (6 oz)
    mozzarella cheese,
    sliced
125 g (4 oz) Parma
    ham, halved
salt and pepper

SAUCE

1 tablespoon olive oil
175 g (6 oz) button
    mushrooms, sliced
5 tablespoons Marsala
2 teaspoons cornflour
3 tablespoons soured
    cream
2 teaspoons chopped
    fresh sage leaves

GARNISH

fresh sage leaves

❶ Place the veal slices between cling film and beat them out until they become thin. If they are large pieces, cut them up so that you have 8 pieces. Season them and place on each a slice of cheese and a piece of Parma ham. Roll up and secure each one with a cocktail stick. Arrange in a basket, cover with a piece of greaseproof paper and steam for 20 minutes.

To make the sauce, heat the oil in a saucepan, add the mushrooms and cook for 4–5 minutes until tender. Pour in the Marsala and simmer for 5 minutes. Blend the cornflour with 3 tablespoons of the cooking juices from the drip tray and add to the pan. Stir the sauce until thickened. Add the soured cream and sage to the sauce and reheat.

Remove the cocktail sticks from the veal rolls and place on a warm serving dish. Pour over the sauce and garnish with sage leaves.

Pork and Prawn Dim Sum

SERVES 6 AS A STARTER

These tasty packets of food are ideally cooked in the steamer and would make a delicious starter to a Chinese meal.

175 g (6 oz) plain
flour, plus extra for
kneading
1 egg yolk
125 ml (4 fl oz) very
hot water

FILLING

175 g (6 oz) minced
pork
125 g (4 oz) peeled
prawns, chopped
1 tablespoon light soy
sauce
2 teaspoons dry sherry
3 spring onions,
chopped finely
1 teaspoon finely
chopped fresh root
ginger
1 teaspoon sesame oil,
plus extra for
greasing
1 small egg (size
4–5), beaten

GARNISH

2 strips of red pepper,
diced finely
spring onion tassels

❶ Put the flour into a large bowl, add the egg yolk and stir in most of the hot water. Work together on a lightly floured surface until the mixture forms a smooth dough, only adding more water if needed. Put the dough back into the bowl, cover and leave to rest for 20 minutes.

Meanwhile put all the ingredients for the filling into a bowl and mix together.

Knead the dough again on a lightly floured surface and then divide into 16–20 pieces. Roll each piece into a ball and then roll out until about 7.5 cm (3 inches) in diameter. Place a heaped teaspoon of the filling in the centre of each round of dough. Bring up the edges, pinching to form little pleats round the side of each dumpling, so that the filling is just left exposed on top.

Scatter a few tiny pieces of red pepper on each dumpling. Place the dumplings in 2 greased baskets and cook for 20 minutes in the steamer.

Garnish with spring onion tassels and serve hot, with extra soy sauce if liked.

Steak Teriyaki
Pork and Prawn Dim
Sum

Steak Teriyaki

SERVES 4

Choose thickly-cut pieces of steak, as lean as possible.

750 g (1½ lb) sirloin
    steak
1 tablespoon
    sunflower oil
2 teaspoons soft light
    brown sugar
4 tablespoons soy
    sauce
5 tablespoons dry
    sherry
2 garlic cloves,
    crushed
1 teaspoon ground
    ginger
1 small head of
    Chinese leaves
125 g (4 oz)
    mangetout,
    chopped

1. Cut the steaks into long thin strips 1 cm (½ inch) wide and 13 cm (5 inches) long; then beat until thin. Mix the oil, sugar, soy sauce, sherry, garlic and ginger together in a bowl. Add the meat and marinate for 1 hour.

Weave the strips of meat on to short bamboo skewers, place in a basket in the steamer, and spoon over half the marinade. Cook for 10 minutes. Spoon over the rest of the marinade.

Shred the Chinese leaves and mix with the mangetout; put them into another basket and place over the meat. Cook both for 3–4 minutes so that the vegetables are just lightly cooked.

Serve the skewers on a bed of the vegetables and spoon a little juice from the drip tray over each portion.

Steak and Kidney Pudding

SERVES 6

750 g (1½ lb)
    braising steak, cut
    into 2.5 cm
    (1-inch) cubes
175 g (6 oz) ox
    kidney, cut into
    1 cm (½-inch)
    cubes
2 tablespoons plain
    flour, seasoned

1. Put the beef and kidney into a bowl, toss in the flour, and add the onion, parsley and stock; stir well and set aside.

Sieve the flour into a bowl and mix with the salt and the suet; add enough of the cold water to mix to a soft dough. Lightly knead the pastry on a floured surface; then roll out three-quarters to a round so that it is 2.5 cm (1 inch) larger than the top of a greased 1.2-litre (2-pint) basin, and 5 mm (¼ inch) thick. Press

1 medium-size onion,
  chopped
1 tablespoon chopped
  fresh parsley
5 tablespoons good
  cold beef stock

PASTRY

300 g (10 oz) self-
  raising flour, plus
  extra for kneading
a pinch of salt
150 g (5 oz) shredded
  suet
175 ml (6 fl oz) water
butter or margarine
  for greasing

GARNISH

sprigs of fresh parsley

well into the basin to remove any creases.

Spoon in the meat mixture and pour in the stock. Roll out the remaining piece of dough to fit the top of the basin. Dampen the edges, place the lid in position and seal. Cover with a pleated sheet of greaseproof paper or foil, secure with string and steam for 2½ hours. Top up the reservoir with boiling water when needed.

Garnish with parsley and serve with green vegetables.

Bacon Pot au Feu
SERVES 6–8

1.5 litres (2½ pints)
  vegetable stock
2 medium-size
  onions, quartered
4 large carrots, sliced
  thickly
3 celery sticks,
  chopped
1 bay leaf
4 black peppercorns
1.5 kg (3½ lb)
  gammon joint
2 turnips, quartered

Put the stock into the reservoir, and add the onions, half the carrots, celery, bay leaf and peppercorns; do not use the drip tray. Place the gammon joint in a basket and cook for 1½ hours.

Put the rest of the carrots and the turnips around the joint and continue to steam for 20 minutes. Serve the gammon sliced, surrounded with the carrots and turnips.

NOTE

If liked, make a parsley sauce with 150 ml (¼ pint) of the stock from the steamer and 150 ml (¼ pint) milk. The stock in the steamer can be used as a basis for a soup.

Clockwise from top left:
Bacon Pot au Feu
Steak and Kidney
Pudding
Lamb Couscous

Lamb Couscous

SERVES 4

Couscous is traditionally cooked in a *couscoussier*, a sort of double boiler. In this recipe the steamer has been adapted to cook this delicious Moroccan dish.

1 kg (2 lb) boned leg of lamb, cut into cubes
2 garlic cloves, crushed
1 green chilli, de-seeded and chopped finely
1 medium-size onion, chopped
75 g (3 oz) chick-peas, soaked overnight
2 tablespoons olive oil
2 teaspoons ground cumin
2 teaspoons paprika
½ teaspoon Cayenne pepper
250 g (8 oz) couscous
300 ml (½ pint) warm water
75 g (3 oz) raisins
¼ teaspoon saffron powder
1 teaspoon ground turmeric
2 teaspoons ground coriander
50 g (2 oz) butter, melted
salt and pepper

🔢 Put the lamb, garlic, chilli, onion and chick-peas into the non-perforated tray and stir in the oil, cumin, paprika and Cayenne pepper. Steam for 1 hour.

Meanwhile put the couscous into a bowl and pour over the warm water. Leave to stand while the meat is cooking, during which time the couscous will swell.

Check the water level in the reservoir, adding more water if necessary. Stir the raisins, saffron, turmeric and coriander into the lamb, season and mix well.

Put the couscous into a basket, place on top of the meat and continue to steam for 30 minutes. Stir the meat mixture and stir the couscous with a fork; then continue to steam both for a further 30 minutes.

Transfer the couscous to a warm serving dish, pour over the melted butter and toss together, breaking up any lumps. Spoon over the meat mixture and serve.

Pork Tenderloin with Sage

SERVES 4

The stuffing imparts a tangy flavour to the pork, which looks really appetising when sliced for serving.

2 pork fillets weighing about 500 g (1 lb) each
25 g (1 oz) butter
1 small onion, chopped finely
1 small cooking apple, peeled, cored and chopped
1 tablespoon chopped fresh sage leaves or 1 teaspoon dried sage
1 teaspoon whole-grain mustard
3 tablespoons double cream
1 teaspoon cornflour
salt and pepper
sprigs of fresh sage, to garnish

❶ With a sharp knife, cut along one side of each fillet and open out. Flatten slightly with a rolling pin and season with salt and pepper.

Melt the butter in a medium-size saucepan and cook the onion until soft. Stir in the apple, cook for 2–3 minutes and add the sage. Spoon this mixture down the centre of each fillet, fold the meat over, and secure it with cocktail sticks or fine string.

Put the pork in a basket and steam for 40 minutes. Pour the juices from the drip tray into a saucepan and boil to reduce to 150 ml (¼ pint); then stir in the mustard. Blend the cream with the cornflour and add it to the sauce, reheating it to thicken.

To serve, remove the cocktail sticks or string from the pork and cut into slices. Arrange these slightly overlapping on warm plates and pour over a little sauce. Garnish with sprigs of sage.

Italian Meatballs in Tomato Sauce
SERVES 4
Serve with spaghetti or rice for a tasty family meal.

MEATBALLS

500 g (1 lb) lean
   minced lamb
50 g (2 oz) fresh
   breadcrumbs
1–2 garlic cloves,
   crushed
2 tablespoons chopped
   fresh parsley
1 shallot, chopped
   finely
1 small egg (size
   4–5), beaten
125 g (4 oz) button
   mushrooms,
   chopped finely
salt and pepper

SAUCE

1 tablespoon olive oil
1 garlic clove, crushed
1 small onion, chopped
   finely
1 red or green pepper,
   de-seeded and
   chopped
400 g (14 oz) can of
   chopped tomatoes
2 teaspoons chopped
   fresh basil or
   1/2 teaspoon dried
   basil
2 teaspoons cornflour
salt and pepper

❶ To make the meatballs, put all the ingredients into a large bowl and mix thoroughly, seasoning with salt and pepper. With wetted hands form the mixture into about 16 balls. Place in a basket in the steamer and cook for 30 minutes.

Meanwhile, make the sauce. Heat the oil in a saucepan, add the garlic, onion and pepper and cook over a low heat until soft. Add the tomatoes and their juice, basil and seasoning, and simmer uncovered for 20 minutes.

Pour the juices from the drip tray into a jug and use 150 ml (1/4 pint) to blend with the cornflour. Add this to the tomato sauce and reheat to thicken. Serve the meatballs with the sauce poured over.

Italian Meatballs in
Tomato Sauce
Citrus Pork Chops

Citrus Pork Chops
SERVES 4

900 ml (1½ pints)
  chicken stock
a pinch of ground
  cloves
a sprig of fresh
  rosemary
grated rind and juice
  of 1 lemon
4 trimmed boneless
  pork loin chops
  weighing about
  200 g (7 oz) each
2 oranges
1 tablespoon oil
2 shallots, chopped
  finely
2 teaspoons cornflour
1 teaspoon soft light
  brown sugar
salt and pepper

Put the stock into the reservoir with the cloves, rosemary and lemon rind and juice.

Place the pork chops in a basket and season with salt and pepper. Cut some thin strips of orange peel from the oranges with a zester and set aside. Remove all the remaining peel and pith from the oranges, cut into segments, and place them over the chops. Steam the chops for about 15 minutes until tender.

Meanwhile put the oil into a saucepan, add the shallots and cook gently until soft. Keeping the chops warm, pour the cooking juice from the drip tray into the saucepan with 450 ml (¾ pint) of the stock from the reservoir, and boil to reduce to 300 ml (½ pint). Blend the cornflour with 2 tablespoons of the stock and add to the pan with the sugar and orange strips. Stir the sauce until it thickens, and season if necessary.

Serve the chops with the sauce poured over them.

Fillets of Beef with Shallots
SERVES 4

4 black peppercorns,
  crushed
750 ml (1¼ pints)
  beef stock
4 fillet steaks
  weighing 125 g
  (4 oz) each
25 g (1 oz) butter

Put the peppercorns into the reservoir with the stock. Place the steaks in a basket and cook for 10 minutes.

Meanwhile, melt the butter in a saucepan and cook the mushrooms and shallots for a few minutes until soft and lightly browned. When the steaks are cooked, add the juices from the drip tray and 150 ml (¼ pint)

125 g (4 oz) button
  mushrooms, sliced
75 g (3 oz) shallots,
  chopped
4 tablespoons crème
  fraiche or soured
  cream
1 tablespoon whisky
salt and pepper
sprigs of fresh
  watercress, to
  garnish

of the stock from the reservoir to the saucepan; boil until reduced by half. Stir in the crème fraiche or soured cream and whisky and reheat, stirring all the time; do not allow to boil. Season, if needed, before transferring the steaks to a warm serving dish and pouring over the sauce. Garnish with sprigs of watercress.

Gammon in Cider
SERVES 4

450 ml (¾ pint) cider
600 ml (1 pint)
  chicken stock
a bouquet garni
1 tablespoon whole-
  grain mustard
25 g (1 oz) demerara
  sugar
4 gammon steaks
  weighing 125 g
  (4 oz) each
15 g (½ oz) butter
25 g (1 oz) plain flour
salt and pepper
chopped fresh parsley,
  to garnish

Pour 300 ml (½ pint) of the cider into the reservoir with the chicken stock, and add the bouquet garni.

Put the mustard and sugar into a bowl and mix to a paste with 2 tablespoons of the remaining cider; spread over the gammon steaks. Arrange the gammon in 2 baskets, place in the steamer, and cook for 15 minutes until tender.

Measure 150 ml (¼ pint) of the juices from the drip tray into a saucepan; add the butter, flour and the rest of the cider, and season. Heat, whisking all the time until a smooth sauce forms, and then simmer for 2 minutes.

Put the gammon steaks on to warm plates and pour over the sauce; sprinkle with chopped parsley and serve.

Surprise Meat Roll

SERVES 4–6

The surprise is in the middle – if liked add some chopped olives to the filling mixture.

750 g (1½ lb) lean minced beef

2 tablespoons tomato purée

1 small onion, chopped very finely

25 g (1 oz) fresh wholemeal breadcrumbs

2 tablespoons chopped fresh parsley

1 egg, beaten

salt and pepper

FILLING

1 tablespoon oil

2 celery sticks, chopped

250 g (8 oz) mushrooms, chopped

1 red pepper, de-seeded and chopped

1 teaspoon dried oregano or 2 teaspoons chopped fresh oregano

salt and pepper

❶ In a large bowl mix the minced beef, tomato purée, onion, breadcrumbs and parsley together. Add the egg, season and mix again.

To make the filling, heat the oil in a saucepan, and add the celery, mushrooms and pepper; cook until the vegetables just begin to soften. Stir in the oregano and season.

Place the meat mixture on a sheet of greaseproof paper and pat out to a rectangle measuring approximately 23 × 30 cm (9 × 12 inches) and about 1½ cm (¾ inch) thick. Spread the filling mixture over the meat mixture; then, using both hands, gently roll up the meat mixture like a swiss roll. Wrap the roll in a fresh piece of greaseproof paper; then place in a basket in the steamer and cook for 50 minutes.

Bobotie

SERVES 4

**This South African dish is quick and easy to prepare.
The minced beef is mixed with fruit and spices to make a tasty dish.**

1 tablespoon oil
1 medium-size onion,
    chopped
500 g (1 lb) lean
    minced beef
1 garlic clove, crushed
1 tablespoon curry
    powder
1 slice of wholemeal
    bread, soaked in
    2 tablespoons water
5 semi-dried apricots,
    chopped
50 g (2 oz) raisins
1 teaspoon dried
    mixed herbs
50 g (2 oz) blanched
    almonds, shredded
1 tablespoon lemon
    juice
1 egg
150 ml (¼ pint) milk
salt and pepper

❶ Heat the oil in a large frying pan. Add the onion and minced beef and cook for about 5 minutes until the onion softens and the mince is browned. Stir in the garlic and curry powder and cook for 2 minutes. Add the bread, apricots and raisins, herbs, almonds and lemon juice, and season well.

Turn the mixture into a pyrex or ovenproof dish approximately 1.5 litres (2½ pints) in capacity. Beat the egg and milk together and pour over the meat. Cover with foil and then place in a basket in the steamer. Cook for 1 hour, or until the mixture is firm. Serve with a salad and crusty bread.

POULTRY DISHES

Herbed Chicken Parcels
SERVES 4

1 teaspoon cornflour
*4 tablespoons natural
    yogurt*
*grated rind of
    1 lemon*
*1 teaspoon Dijon
    mustard*
*1 teaspoon coriander
    seeds, crushed*
*4 boneless chicken
    breasts weighing
    175 g (6 oz) each,
    skinned*
*2 tablespoons chopped
    fresh parsley*
*1 tablespoon chopped
    fresh thyme*
*1 tablespoon chopped
    fresh basil*
*1 tablespoon chopped
    fresh chives*
salt and pepper
*sprigs of fresh thyme,
    to garnish*

❶ In a small bowl blend the cornflour with the yogurt, and add the lemon rind, mustard and coriander; mix until smooth.

Put the chicken breasts in a dish and coat with the yogurt marinade; cover and refrigerate for 2–3 hours. Place each chicken breast on a piece of foil, season with salt and pepper and spoon over any remaining marinade. Sprinkle over the freshly chopped herbs. Wrap up the chicken to make into parcels. Place in a basket in the steamer and cook for 20–25 minutes.

To serve, place each parcel on a warm plate and fold back the foil. Garnish with sprigs of thyme.

Turkey Rolls with Cranberry and Vermouth

SERVES 4

Turkey escalopes come in various sizes, so you will need to use your judgement when cutting them up to give 12 pieces.

900 ml (1½ pints) chicken stock
a bouquet garni
375 g (12 oz) turkey escalopes
4 large slices of smoked ham
190 g (6½ oz) cranberry sauce
5 tablespoons vermouth or dry white wine
15 g (½ oz) butter
15 g (½ oz) plain flour

Pour the stock into the reservoir and add the bouquet garni.

In turn, put each turkey escalope between cling film and beat it until thin. If large, cut up to give 12 pieces. Cut each slice of ham into 3 and lay a portion on each piece of turkey. Place a teaspoon of cranberry sauce on top, roll up and secure with a cocktail stick.

Put the turkey rolls into a basket in the steamer and cook for 20 minutes. Pour the cooking liquid from the drip tray into a saucepan and then return the turkey to the steamer to keep warm while making the sauce.

Boil the juices in the saucepan to reduce to 150 ml (¼ pint). Then add the remaining cranberry sauce and vermouth or wine, and simmer for 5 minutes. Meanwhile mash the butter and flour together on a small plate and add to the sauce a little at a time, stirring the sauce continuously. Season if needed.

To serve, arrange the turkey rolls on warm plates and pour over the sauce.

Clockwise from top:
Herbed Chicken
Parcels
Turkey Rolls with
Cranberry and
Vermouth
Duck with
Blackcurrants

Duck with Blackcurrants

SERVES 4

Boneless duck breasts are available in most large supermarkets. They can be cooked quickly to retain flavour and succulence.

4 boneless duck breasts weighing 175 g (6 oz) each, skinned
2 tablespoons red wine
150 ml (¼ pint) chicken stock
2 tablespoons black-currant conserve
2 teaspoons cornflour
25 g (1 oz) black-currants, thawed if frozen (optional)
salt and pepper
fresh mint leaves, to garnish

❶ Season the duck breasts. Then place them in a basket in the steamer, sprinkle over the wine, and cook for 15 minutes.

While the duck is cooking, put the chicken stock in a pan with the blackcurrant conserve and simmer until the mixture is reduced and has a syrupy consistency.

Measure 150 ml (¼ pint) of the juices from the drip tray into a jug, blend with the cornflour and then add to the pan with the whole blackcurrants, if used. Allow to simmer while slicing the duck breasts and arranging them on warmed plates.

Season the sauce if needed and then pour the hot sauce over the duck and garnish with mint leaves. Serve at once.

Chicken Liver Pâté

SERVES 4–6

500 g (1 lb) chicken livers
1 garlic clove, crushed
1 small onion, chopped finely
125 g (4 oz) butter
3 tablespoons double cream
¼ teaspoon grated nutmeg
2 tablespoons brandy

❷ Clean the chicken livers, trimming away any membranes; then place in the non-perforated tray with the garlic and onion and steam for 10–12 minutes, or until they are firm but still slightly pink inside. Drain away any excess liquid.

Put the mixture into a food processor with the rest of the ingredients and work until it is smooth; season with salt and pepper. Spoon the pâté into a terrine dish and smooth the top; when cool, cover and refrigerate for

or dry sherry
salt and pepper
sprigs of fresh chervil
or parsley,
to garnish

at least 6 hours. Serve with melba toast, garnished with chervil or parsley.

Oriental Chicken

SERVES 4

This kind of dish can be varied by using different vegetables such as broccoli florets, finely sliced carrot or shredded leeks.

3 boneless chicken breasts weighing 150–175 g (5–6 oz) each, skinned
2.5 cm (1-inch) piece of fresh root ginger, peeled and chopped finely
1 garlic clove, crushed
3 spring onions, shredded
125 g (4 oz) mangetout, halved
50 g (2 oz) bean sprouts, trimmed
1 red pepper, de-seeded and sliced finely
1 tablespoon soy sauce
1 tablespoon dry sherry
2 teaspoons cornflour

① Cut the chicken into thin strips and put these into a basket in the steamer to cook for 3 minutes. Add the ginger, garlic and vegetables and cook for a further 6 minutes.

Pour the cooking juices from the drip tray into a jug; then return the chicken to the steamer to keep warm while making the sauce.

In a small saucepan blend the soy sauce, sherry and cornflour together; gradually blend in 150 ml (¼ pint) of the cooking juices and then bring to the boil to thicken.

Put the chicken into a warm serving dish and pour over the sauce. Serve at once, with noodles.

Clockwise from top:
Kashmir Chicken
Honey Gingered
Duck
Oriental Chicken

Honey Gingered Duck

SERVES 4

Removing the skin from duck breasts avoids the fatty flavour that is often associated with duck and makes for a more elegant dish.

5 star anise
a large knob of fresh root ginger, peeled and sliced
4 boneless duck breasts weighing 175 g (6 oz) each, skinned
1 tablespoon clear honey
2 teaspoons lemon juice
1 tablespoon dry sherry
2 teaspoons soy sauce
spring onion tassels, to garnish

❶ Add the star anise to the reservoir. Place the ginger in a basket; lay the duck breasts on the ginger and cook for 15 minutes.

Measure 150 ml (¼ pint) of the cooking juices from the drip tray and pour into a saucepan; return the duck to the steamer to keep warm. Bring the liquid to the boil and add the honey, lemon juice, sherry and soy sauce. Boil for about 5 minutes to reduce by about half.

Cut each duck breast into slices, arrange on warmed plates and drizzle over the sauce. Garnish each with a spring onion tassel.

Kashmir Chicken

SERVES 4

A deliciously fragrant dish; serve with pilau rice and Indian chutney for a memorable meal.

4 boneless chicken breasts weighing about 175 g (6 oz) each, skinned
150 ml (¼ pint) natural yogurt
1 teaspoon ground cumin
1 teaspoon ground coriander

❶ Cut the chicken into 2.5 cm (1-inch) cubes. In a glass dish mix the yogurt, spices and garlic together, adding a little salt. Cover and marinate overnight.

Line a basket with some of the coriander leaves and place the chicken pieces on top. Cook for 15–20 minutes until the chicken is tender.

Meanwhile, dissolve the creamed coconut in the hot chicken stock. Heat the oil

1 teaspoon ground
   turmeric
1/2 teaspoon ground
   ginger
1/4 teaspoon chilli
   powder
1 garlic clove, crushed
a large bunch of fresh
   coriander leaves
25 g (1 oz) creamed
   coconut
5 tablespoons hot
   chicken stock
1 tablespoon oil
1 small onion,
   chopped finely
1 tablespoon plain
   flour
salt

in a medium-size saucepan, add the onion and cook until soft; stir in the flour and then gradually add the dissolved coconut. Stir in the cooking juices from the drip tray and simmer for 2 minutes. Chop up 1 tablespoon of the remaining coriander and add this to the sauce.

Serve the pieces of chicken with the sauce, garnished with any remaining coriander leaves.

Spinach Wrapped Chicken Breasts
SERVES 4
Here is a really healthy version of Chicken Kiev; the chicken is succulent and the spinach makes a colourful contrast when the chicken is cut.

12 large fresh spinach
   leaves
4 boneless chicken
   breasts weighing
   150–175 g (5–6 oz)
   each, skinned
70 g (2¾ oz) Boursin
   (soft cheese with
   garlic and herbs)
a little oil for
   brushing
salt and pepper

❶ Trim the spinach leaves, put them into a basket and steam for 4–5 minutes until wilted.

With a sharp knife make a deep cut in each chicken breast to form a pocket. Divide the cheese between them, pressing it into the pockets, and then season. Lay 3 spinach leaves slightly overlapping on a flat surface, and use them to wrap up a chicken breast; repeat this with the rest. Then brush them with oil.

Place the chicken in a basket in the steamer and cook for 45 minutes.

Turkey Provençale

SERVES 4

This is a winning combination – low in calories and full of flavour.

500 g (1 lb) turkey breast fillets
1 small onion, chopped finely
1 garlic clove, crushed
1 red pepper, de-seeded and diced
125 g (4 oz) mushrooms, quartered
1 tablespoon cornflour
125 ml (4 fl oz) dry white wine
4 tomatoes, skinned and chopped
2 teaspoons tomato purée
1/2 teaspoon dried oregano
6 pitted black olives
salt and pepper

❶ Cut the turkey into large chunks and put it into a dish that will fit in the steamer. Mix in the onion, garlic, pepper and mushrooms.

Blend the cornflour with the wine, and pour it into the dish; then stir in the tomatoes, tomato purée and oregano. Season before covering the dish with foil and placing it in a basket in the steamer. Cook for 1 hour.

Just before serving, stir in the olives and season again if necessary. Serve with a mixed salad.

Turkey Provençale
Chicken Véronique

Chicken Véronique
SERVES 4

4 boneless chicken
    breasts weighing
    175 g (6 oz) each,
    skinned
1 teaspoon grated
    lemon rind
125 g (4 oz) green
    grapes
2 tablespoons white
    wine
2 teaspoons cornflour
4 tablespoons natural
    yogurt
salt and pepper

❶ Place the chicken in baskets, season with salt and pepper and scatter over the lemon rind. Place the baskets in the steamer and cook for 20–25 minutes. Transfer to a serving dish and keep warm.

Pour the juices from the drip tray into a saucepan, and boil until reduced by half. Meanwhile place the grapes in the steamer for a few minutes to scald the skins, making peeling easier. Remove the skins and pips from the grapes.

Blend the wine with the cornflour and stir into the saucepan; continue to boil, stirring, until thickened. Take off the heat and stir in the yogurt and grapes; pour the mixture over the chicken and serve.

Country Chicken
SERVES 4

1.5 kg (3½ lb)
    chicken
1 lemon, quartered
a handful of fresh
    parsley
1 small onion,
    quartered
1.2 litres (2 pints)
    chicken stock
a bouquet garni
150 ml (¼ pint) dry
    white wine
salt and pepper

Season the chicken inside and out and then put the lemon, parsley and onion into the body cavity.

Pour the stock into the reservoir, and add the bouquet garni and wine. (Do not use the drip tray.) Place the chicken in a basket and then cook for 60–70 minutes, or until tender.

NOTE

If liked, the stock can be boiled to reduce and then used to make a sauce. Use the carcass to make stock.

STOCKS

Stocks have always been important in cooking, adding both flavour and moisture to dishes. In many recipes in this book, stocks are recommended for use as the steaming liquid rather than water.

The juices collected in the drip tray are ideal for the preparation of sauces, being a combination of the juices of the food being steamed and the stock in the reservoir below. Sauces made this way not only taste delicious, but are full of the natural goodness of the food cooked in the steamer.

Poultry Stock

1 chicken carcass and giblets, except the liver
2 carrots, chopped roughly
1 onion, quartered
1 celery stick, chopped
a bouquet garni
1 garlic clove
1 teaspoon black peppercorns
salt

Break up the carcass and place it in the reservoir of the steamer, avoiding the central core area. Fill the reservoir with water up to the maximum mark, place the tray holder in position and cover. Turn on the steamer and, when boiling, remove the scum from the surface. Add the rest of the ingredients; return the tray holder and lid. Cook the stock for 45 minutes.

Strain the stock through a sieve and use in the preparation of a sauce, or as the steaming liquid when cooking another dish.

Veal Stock

750 g (1½ lb) veal bones
3 carrots, chopped roughly
1 onion, sliced
1 garlic clove
a bouquet garni
salt

Place the bones in a roasting tin and brown in a hot oven for 20–25 minutes.

Next place the bones in the reservoir, avoiding the central core, and add water to come up to the maximum mark. Position the tray holder and lid. Turn on the steamer and bring the liquid to the boil. Remove the scum from the surface of the stock, add the rest of the ingredients, seasoning with salt, and replace the tray holder and lid.

Boil for 2 hours, adding additional water to the reservoir as necessary. At the end of cooking, the stock should be reduced to approximately 600 ml (1 pint).

Strain through a sieve and use in the preparation of a sauce, or as the steaming liquid in another dish.

BEEF STOCK

This can be made in the same way as veal stock by using beef bones and the addition of a 500 g (1 lb) shin of beef, which needs to be browned in the oven with the bones to give the stock a good colour.

Court Bouillon

This is a general purpose stock, suitable for most fish and shellfish dishes.

1 large onion, chopped
2 large carrots, chopped
1 celery stick, chopped
a bunch of fresh parsley
2 garlic cloves
a bouquet garni
1 leek, white part only, chopped
5 black peppercorns
2 coriander seeds
2 teaspoons salt
150 ml (¼ pint) dry white wine (optional)

Place all the ingredients, except the wine (if used), in the reservoir and fill to the maximum level with water. Position the tray holder and lid. Bring to the boil and cook for 10 minutes. If liked, add the wine and cook for a further 5 minutes.

Strain the stock through a sieve and use to steam fish.

EGG AND CHEESE DISHES

Cheese and Courgette Custard
SERVES 4
Make this dish when small, young courgettes are available.

375 g (12 oz)
    courgettes
125 g (4 oz) low-fat
    soft cheese
50 g (2 oz) Cheddar
    cheese, grated finely
2 eggs, beaten lightly
150 ml (¼ pint) milk
2 tablespoons chopped
    fresh chives or
    2 teaspoons dried
    chives
butter for greasing
salt and pepper

❶ Reserve 2 courgettes. Then cut the rest lengthways, removing and discarding the seeds, and grate them coarsely. Sprinkle them with salt, spread on a double layer of kitchen paper and set aside for 30 minutes. Squeeze out as much water as possible.

With a sharp knife, thinly slice the reserved courgettes lengthways. Mix the grated courgettes with the rest of the ingredients, season if needed, and turn into a greased oval *gratin* dish. Arrange the thin slices on top; then cover with greased greaseproof paper, place in a basket and steam for 20–25 minutes until set.

Cheese Ramekins
SERVES 4

2 slices of bread,
    crusts removed
25 g (1 oz) butter,
    plus extra for
    greasing
8 anchovy fillets,
    chopped
2 eggs
50 g (2 oz) Cheddar
    cheese, grated
150 ml (¼ pint) milk
salt, pepper and
    paprika

❶ Cut the bread into small cubes. Melt the butter in a small frying pan and fry the bread cubes until crisp. Divide between 4 greased ramekin dishes; then scatter the chopped anchovies over.

Beat the eggs, cheese and milk together, seasoning with salt and pepper. Pour into the dishes until each one is three-quarters full, place in a basket in the steamer, and then cover with greased greaseproof paper. Steam for 15 minutes or until set. Dust the tops with paprika before serving as a light lunch or supper.

Sesame Omelette

SERVES 1

The filling for this omelette can be varied by adding grated cheese, diced tomatoes, chopped herbs or cooked mushrooms.

1 spring onion, shredded
1 baby courgette, cut into julienne slices
1 baby carrot, cut into julienne slices
1 teaspoon oil for greasing
2 eggs, beaten
1 tablespoon sesame seeds, toasted
salt and pepper

Put the vegetables into a basket.

Line another basket with greaseproof paper so that it comes up the sides, and brush with the oil. Season the eggs and pour in.

Place both baskets in the steamer and cook for 3 minutes, when the egg should be set but still soft on top. Lift the omelette out of the basket, sprinkle over half the sesame seeds, and then cover with the vegetables. Using a palette knife, ease the omelette away from the paper and either fold over or roll up like a swiss roll. Sprinkle with the rest of the sesame seeds and serve immediately.

Smoked Salmon Scramble

SERVES 4

If you like, heart-shaped pieces of toast give this classic dish a new look.

25 g (1 oz) butter
8 eggs
125 g (4 oz) smoked salmon, cut into strips
salt and pepper
sprigs of fresh dill, to garnish

Put the butter into the non-perforated tray and place in the steamer to melt. Beat the eggs, and season with salt and pepper. Pour into the tray and steam for 3–4 minutes, until beginning to set. Stir, and then add the strips of smoked salmon and continue to cook for a further 3–4 minutes, until lightly cooked. Spoon on to warm serving plates and garnish with dill. Serve with toast.

Egg and Spinach Nests

SERVES 4

These are quick and easy to prepare. If fresh spinach is unavailable, 250 g (8 oz) of frozen spinach can be used; make sure that it is well drained when thawed.

500 g (1 lb) spinach, trimmed
25 g (1 oz) butter, plus extra for greasing
4 eggs
15 g (½ oz) parmesan cheese, grated
salt, pepper and Cayenne pepper

Grease 4 individual small *gratin* dishes or ramekins.

Put the spinach in a basket and cook in the steamer for 4–5 minutes until wilted. Remove and roughly chop, put into a bowl, add the butter and seasoning and toss together. Divide between the 4 dishes, pushing it to the edges to make a well in the middle. Break an egg into each dish.

Place in 2 baskets in the steamer and cover with buttered greaseproof paper. Steam for 4 minutes, until the whites begin to set. Sprinkle with the cheese and return to the steamer to cook for a further 2 minutes.

Dust with a little Cayenne pepper before serving.

Clockwise from top:
Smoked Salmon
Scramble
Egg and Spinach
Nests
Sesame Omelette

Piperade

SERVES 2

This colourful egg dish can be served as a light lunch or supper dish.

1 small onion, sliced
1 garlic clove, crushed
1/2 green pepper, de-
    seeded and sliced
1/2 red pepper, de-
    seeded and sliced
butter for greasing
1 large tomato,
    skinned and
    chopped
1/2 teaspoon dried
    mixed herbs
4 eggs, beaten
salt and pepper
chopped fresh parsley,
    to garnish

❶ Put the onion, garlic and peppers into the non-perforated tray and cook in the steamer for 10 minutes. Turn into a buttered *gratin* dish that will fit into the steamer and stir in the tomato and herbs.

Beat the eggs, season with salt and pepper and then pour into the dish. Cover with buttered greaseproof paper, place in a basket and steam for 15 minutes until the eggs have set. Serve garnished with parsley.

Hot Mushroom Mousse

SERVES 6

Serve this mousse with a mixed green salad, for a delicious vegetarian meal.

375 g (12 oz) cup
    mushrooms
40 g (1 1/2 oz) butter,
    plus extra for
    greasing
6 spring onions,
    chopped finely
175 g (6 oz) cottage
    cheese
3 eggs, separated
1 teaspoon lemon
    juice

❶ Grease a 1 kg (2 lb) loaf tin and line with greased greaseproof paper.

Slice 6 of the mushrooms and arrange on the base of the tin. Chop the rest. Melt the butter in a saucepan, add the chopped mushrooms and spring onions and cook for 3 minutes, until softened; cool. Put into a food processor, with the cottage cheese and egg yolks, and work to a purée. Transfer the mixture to a bowl.

Whisk the egg whites until stiff. Fold into the mushroom mixture, with the lemon

2 teaspoons chopped
    fresh tarragon or
    1 teaspoon dried
    tarragon
1 tablespoon chopped
    fresh parsley
salt and pepper

juice, tarragon and parsley, and season with salt and pepper. Turn into the loaf tin, cover with greased foil or greaseproof paper and place in a basket in the steamer. Cook for 20 minutes or until firm; then leave in the steamer for 5 minutes. Turn out on to a serving plate, peel off the lining paper and serve immediately.

Cheese and Ham Mousseline

SERVES 4

This recipe can be varied to include chicken or prawns in place of the ham.

butter for greasing
125 g (4 oz) Cheddar
    cheese, grated
125 g (4 oz) ham,
    minced or chopped
    finely
75 g (3 oz) fresh
    wholemeal
    breadcrumbs
1 teaspoon Dijon
    mustard
2 eggs
300 ml (½ pint) milk
salt and pepper
chopped fresh parsley,
    to garnish

❶ Butter a 15 cm (6-inch) soufflé dish.

Put the cheese, ham, breadcrumbs, mustard and seasoning into a bowl and mix together. Beat the eggs and milk together, and then stir into the cheese mixture. Pour into the dish and cover with greased greaseproof paper. Place in a basket and steam for 50 minutes, or until set.

To serve, turn out on to a warm serving plate and garnish with parsley.

VEGETABLE DISHES

Devilled Potatoes
SERVES 6

This dish would make a good accompaniment to barbecued food. It is also delicious made with a mixture of potatoes and parsnips.

1 kg (2 lb) potatoes, peeled
1 tablespoon plain flour
1 tablespoon mild curry powder
25 g (1 oz) butter
175 ml (6 fl oz) single cream
1 tablespoon chopped fresh parsley

❶ Cut the potatoes in half lengthways, put them in a basket and steam for 20 minutes. They should be steamed *al dente*.

Remove them from the steamer and cut into 2.5 cm (1-inch) cubes. Dust them with the flour and toss them in the curry powder. Place the cubes in the non-perforated tray and dot with the butter. Then pour over the cream, return to the steamer and cook for a further 25 minutes. Before serving, sprinkle with the chopped parsley.

Petits Pois à la Française
SERVES 4–6

A classic dish from France; serve with grilled meat or fish dishes.

500 g (1 lb) shelled small fresh garden peas
½ small cos lettuce, shredded
10 spring onions, chopped
3 teaspoons sugar
25 g (1 oz) butter
salt

❷ Put the peas, lettuce and onions into the non-perforated tray; sprinkle over the sugar and dot with some of the butter. Steam for 15 minutes until the peas are tender. Season with salt; then turn into a warm serving dish and dot with the remaining butter.

Devilled Potatoes
Petits Pois à la
Française
Cauliflower with
Almonds

Cauliflower with Almonds
SERVES 6–8

1 large cauliflower
40 g (1½ oz) butter
50 g (2 oz) blanched
  almonds, slivered
50 g (2 oz) fresh
  breadcrumbs

❶ Break the cauliflower into florets and put them into a basket, stalk ends facing downwards. Steam for 20 minutes or until tender.

Meanwhile, melt the butter in a saucepan and add the almonds and breadcrumbs. Stir over a moderate heat until golden brown.

Transfer the cauliflower to a warm serving dish and spoon over the almonds and breadcrumbs.

Rice Balls
MAKES 8–10

This is a useful recipe which could use up some leftover cooked rice. If liked, rice balls can be served with a tomato sauce to make a more colourful dish.

175 g (6 oz) cooked
  brown rice
50 g (2 oz) Cheddar
  cheese, grated
1 egg, beaten
25 g (1 oz) ground
  almonds
butter for greasing
salt and pepper

❶ Put all the ingredients into a bowl, season and mix thoroughly. Using a dessert spoon take a scoop of the rice mixture; then press it together, using your hands, to form a ball. Place in a greased basket and then repeat the process with the rest of the mixture. Cook the rice balls in the steamer for 20 minutes.

Spinach Creams
SERVES 6

1 kg (2 lb) spinach
40 g (1½ oz) butter,
plus extra for
greasing
¼ teaspoon grated
nutmeg
25 g (1 oz) plain flour
300 ml (½ pint) milk
2 eggs
salt and pepper

❶ Remove the stalks from the spinach, put the leaves in a basket in the steamer, and cook for 5 minutes until wilted. Line 6 buttered ramekins with the leaves, making sure that there are no gaps. Finely chop the rest of the spinach in a food processor or blender. Melt 15 g (½ oz) of the butter in a saucepan, add the spinach and nutmeg and season with salt and pepper.

Melt the remaining butter in a saucepan, add the flour and cook for 1 minute. Gradually add the milk and cook, stirring constantly until the sauce begins to thicken. Add the spinach mixture to the sauce and then remove from the heat. Beat in the eggs and season if necessary.

Spoon the mixture into the prepared ramekins until each one is three-quarters full; then cover them with lids of foil. Steam in baskets for 20 minutes until set. Turn the creams out of the ramekins on to a warm serving dish and serve.

Vegetable Jardinière with Piquant Dip
SERVES 4–6
The steamer is ideal for making this dish: the vegetables retain all their shape, colour, texture and nutrients. Blanch all the vegetables together in one go.

½ cauliflower, cut into florets
3 large carrots, cut into sticks
125 g (4 oz) whole green beans
125 g (4 oz) button mushrooms
175 g (6 oz) baby sweetcorn
175 g (6 oz) cherry tomatoes

DIP
125 g (4 oz) low-fat soft cheese
150 ml (¼ pint) soured cream
4 tablespoons tomato ketchup
1 teaspoon horseradish sauce
1 teaspoon Worcestershire sauce
1 garlic clove, crushed
1 teaspoon French mustard
a dash of Tabasco sauce

❶ Arrange the cauliflower, carrots, beans, mushrooms and sweetcorn in baskets and cook for 3–4 minutes to blanch them. Cool the vegetables under cold running water and then arrange them on a serving platter, with the tomatoes.

To make the dip, put the cheese, cream and ketchup into a bowl and beat them together until smooth. Stir in the rest of the ingredients and mix thoroughly. Chill before serving with the vegetables.

*Vegetable Jardinière
with Piquant Dip*

Asparagus with Hollandaise Sauce
SERVES 4

4 tablespoons white
  wine vinegar
6 black peppercorns
1 blade of mace
1 slice of onion
1 bay leaf
3 egg yolks
150 g (5 oz) soft
  unsalted butter
1 tablespoon single
  cream
375 g (12 oz)
  asparagus
pepper

❶ To make the sauce, put the vinegar into a saucepan with the spices, onion and bay leaf. Boil until only 1 tablespoon of liquid remains, and set this aside.

Put the egg yolks into a bowl and beat in 1 tablespoon of the butter. Add the vinegar mixture and then place the bowl over a pan of boiling water. When the mixture blends, turn off the heat and whisk in the remaining butter – a little at a time – until the sauce is shiny and has the consistency of thick cream. Before serving, season with pepper, and add the cream.

Cut the woody ends off the asparagus and scrape off the scales. Put the prepared asparagus into a basket and cook for 10–15 minutes until the green stalks are tender. Serve the asparagus hot with the sauce poured over, or serve with a separate bowl of hollandaise sauce for each serving.

Spinach and Carrot Timbales
SERVES 6
These dainty vegetable mounds make a very sophisticated accompaniment to a dinner party meal; try using broccoli instead of spinach as a variation.

butter for greasing
750 g (1½ lb) carrots,
  chopped
250 g (8 oz) spinach,
  trimmed
1 egg, beaten
a pinch of grated
  nutmeg

❶ Grease 6 dariole moulds or ramekin dishes.

Cook the carrots in a basket in the steamer for 15 minutes until they are tender. Then chop them finely in a blender or food processor, and transfer to a bowl.

Put the spinach into a basket in the steamer and cook for 2 minutes or until the leaves are wilted. Drain very well and chop in

salt and pepper
sprigs of fresh
    rosemary,
    to garnish

the blender or food processor. Add the chopped leaves to the carrots with the egg and nutmeg and season well.

Spoon the mixture into the moulds, pressing down slightly. Then place the moulds in a basket in the steamer and cover with greased greaseproof paper. Cook for 20 minutes or until set.

To serve, run a knife round the edge of each mould, turn out on to a warm serving plate and garnish with rosemary.

Leeks with Ham in Parsley Sauce
SERVES 4

8 medium-size leeks
8 slices of ham
50 g (2 oz) Cheddar
    cheese, grated
SAUCE
25 g (1 oz) butter
25 g (1 oz) plain
    flour
300 ml (½ pint) milk
3 tablespoons chopped
    fresh parsley
salt and pepper

❶ Put the leeks into a basket and cook for 20 minutes. Preheat the oven to Gas Mark 5/190°C/375°F.

Meanwhile, make the sauce. Melt the butter in a saucepan, add the flour and cook for 1 minute. Gradually add the milk, stirring constantly until the sauce thickens. Add the parsley and season to taste.

Wrap each leek in a slice of ham and lay it in an ovenproof dish. Pour the sauce over the leeks; then sprinkle with the cheese and bake for 20 minutes in the oven.

Clockwise from top:
Asparagus with
Hollandaise Sauce
Spinach and Carrot
Timbales
Leeks with Ham in
Parsley Sauce

Stuffed Peppers
SERVES 4

40 g (1½ oz) butter
1 small onion,
    chopped finely
125 g (4 oz) long-
    grain rice
50 g (2 oz)
    mushrooms,
    chopped
450 ml (¾ pint)
    vegetable or
    chicken stock
125 g (4 oz) cooked
    ham, diced
a good pinch of dried
    mixed herbs
4 red, yellow or green
    peppers
salt and pepper
sprigs of fresh flat-
    leafed parsley, to
    garnish

❶ Melt the butter in a saucepan, add the onion and cook until soft. Stir in the rice and mushrooms; then add the stock, bring to the boil and simmer for 15 minutes until the rice is just cooked and the stock absorbed. Add the ham and herbs and season.

Cut the tops off the peppers and remove the cores and seeds. Stuff the peppers with the mixture and replace the tops; then stand them in a basket and cover with a piece of greaseproof paper. Steam for 25 minutes, until the peppers are tender. Serve garnished with parsley.

Spaghetti Squash with Pesto Sauce
SERVES 4
It is worth looking out for this unusual vegetable; when the cooked flesh is scooped out it looks just like spaghetti! If children find the flavour of the pesto sauce rather pungent, substitute a tomato sauce.

1 medium-size
    spaghetti squash
PESTO SAUCE
25 g (1 oz) fresh basil
    leaves
2 garlic cloves

❶ Cut the squash in half and remove the seeds. Place the halves cut-side down in a basket. Steam for 20 minutes.

To make the sauce, put the basil leaves, garlic, oil and pine kernels into a blender or food processor and work until smooth. Scrape

4 tablespoons olive oil
2 tablespoons pine
  kernels
4 tablespoons double
  cream
40 g (1½ oz)
  parmesan cheese,
  grated
GARNISH
fresh basil leaves

out into a bowl and stir in the cream and half the cheese.

To test whether the squash is cooked, take a fork and gently pull away the flesh; it should come away in strands. Add these to the pesto sauce and toss them together. Turn the mixture into an ovenproof *gratin* dish. Sprinkle over the rest of the cheese and place under a hot grill until golden brown. Garnish with basil.

Ratatouille
SERVES 6–8

With the variety of vegetables used to make this tasty dish, it is difficult to make a small amount, so serve any left over as a salad.

1 small aubergine
2 tablespoons olive oil
1 large onion, sliced
1–2 garlic cloves,
  crushed
1 green pepper, de-
  seeded and sliced
1 red pepper, de-
  seeded and sliced
250 g (8 oz)
  courgettes, sliced
375 g (12 oz)
  tomatoes, skinned
  and chopped
2 tablespoons tomato
  purée
1 teaspoon dried
  oregano
1 tablespoon chopped
  fresh parsley
salt and pepper

❶ Cut the aubergine into small cubes, put these into a colander and sprinkle with salt. Leave for 30 minutes; then rinse and pat dry with kitchen paper.

Put the oil into a frying pan, add the onion and cook over a moderate heat until soft. Add the remaining ingredients, except for the parsley, season and then transfer to the non-perforated tray. Place in the steamer and cook for 1 hour until the vegetables are tender. Stir in the parsley before serving.

Clockwise from top:
Spaghetti Squash with
Pesto Sauce
Ratatouille
Stuffed Peppers

Stuffed Cabbage

SERVES 4 AS A LIGHT MEAL OR 8 AS AN ACCOMPANIMENT

A colourful selection of vegetables inside these parcels makes a change from the usual stuffing for cabbage leaves.

50 g (2 oz) bulgur wheat
2 tomatoes, skinned, de-seeded and diced
8 large green cabbage leaves
125 g (4 oz) fine green beans
1 large carrot, cut into thin strips
2 courgettes, cut into thin strips
1 red pepper, de-seeded and cut into strips
salt and pepper

❶ Put the bulgur wheat into a bowl, pour over some warm water and leave to soak for 5 minutes. Drain, squeezing out any excess liquid, and put into a bowl with the tomatoes; season and set aside.

Cut away the coarse part of the cabbage leaves near the centre rib; then put the leaves into a basket and steam until limp. Refresh with cold water and drain.

Put the green beans and carrot into a basket and steam for 2 minutes. Then add the courgettes and pepper strips and steam for a further 2 minutes.

To stuff each leaf, lay it out flat and add some of the blanched vegetables. Make sure there are some of each type of vegetable. Then add 2 teaspoons of the bulgur mixture. Roll up the leaf, folding in the sides to make a neat parcel, and place in a basket. Repeat with the rest of the leaves and filling. Steam the cabbage parcels for 15 minutes. Serve with tomato sauce (page 36).

Tamale Pie

SERVES 4

This Mexican flavoured dish has a crust made from cornmeal and a bean filling that would make a spicy vegetarian meal.

butter for greasing
250 g (8 oz) cornmeal
4 tablespoons oil
a large pinch of salt

❶ Grease a 750 ml (1¼-pint) oval pie dish.
Put the cornmeal into a bowl with 3 tablespoons of the oil, the salt and the cheese. Add the hot water and stir well; then

125 g (4 oz) Cheddar
    cheese, grated
200 ml (7 fl oz) hot
    water
1 large onion,
    chopped
3 celery sticks,
    chopped
½ green pepper, de-
    seeded and
    chopped
1 garlic clove, crushed
1 teaspoon chilli
    powder
2 tablespoons tomato
    purée
400 g (14 oz) can of
    red kidney beans,
    drained

mix with the fingertips to make a soft dough.

Press two-thirds of the dough inside the dish, spreading it evenly with your fingers, as it will have a crumbly texture.

Heat the remaining oil in a frying pan, add the onion and fry gently for 5 minutes until soft and lightly coloured. Add the celery and pepper and continue to cook for 5 minutes. Stir in the garlic and chilli powder and cook for 1 minute. Add the tomato purée and beans and mix well. Spoon the mixture into the dish.

Cover with the rest of the cornmeal dough, trying to spread it as evenly as possible and pressing down to level the surface. Cover the pie with greased foil or greaseproof paper, place in a basket and steam for 40 minutes. Serve with a crisp salad.

Mushroom Tagliatelle
SERVES 4
This simply prepared dish would make a good meal for a light lunch or supper. It can be varied adding strips of ham, chopped nuts, clams or prawns.

275 g (9 oz)
    tagliatelle
1 tablespoon olive oil
1 garlic clove, crushed
250 g (8 oz)
    mushrooms, sliced
150 ml (¼ pint)
    soured cream
2 tablespoons chopped
    fresh parsley
salt and pepper

❷ Bring a saucepan of water to the boil, add the tagliatelle and cook for 5 minutes. Drain and then toss the pasta in the oil. Add the garlic and mushrooms and place in a basket in the steamer to cook for 6 minutes.

Turn into a warm dish and season with salt and pepper. Then stir in the cream and parsley.

DESSERTS AND CAKES

Mulled Fruit Salad

SERVES 6

Perfect for winter days when served warm, and equally delicious eaten cold with whipped cream.

150 ml (¼ pint) sweet cider

6 tablespoons clear honey

a 2.5 cm (1-inch) piece of fresh root ginger, peeled

a stick of cinnamon

8 plums, halved and stoned

2 apples, cored and sliced

2 oranges, peeled and segmented

2 pears, peeled and quartered

2 apricots, halved and stoned

2 peaches, skinned, stoned and sliced

2 bananas, peeled and cut into chunks

1 kiwi fruit, peeled and sliced

8 maraschino cherries (optional)

2 tablespoons lemon juice

1 Put the cider, honey, ginger and cinnamon stick into the non-perforated tray and place in the steamer. Allow to cook for 5 minutes, stirring to dissolve the honey.

Meanwhile toss the prepared fruit in the lemon juice to prevent discoloration. Add to the syrup in the steamer and steam for 10–15 minutes until softened.

Put into a serving bowl and serve warm, or allow to cool, cover and chill before serving.

Mulled Fruit Salad
Banana Parcels

Banana Parcels

SERVES 4

A delicious way to cook bananas; if making them for children omit the liqueur and use fruit juice instead.

4 tablespoons apricot
  jam
4 teaspoons caster
  sugar
2 tablespoons
  Amaretto liqueur
1 tablespoon lemon
  juice
1 tablespoon water
1 teaspoon vanilla
  essence
4 large bananas
butter for greasing

🍌 Place the jam, sugar, liqueur, lemon juice, water and vanilla essence in a small saucepan and heat gently until the jam melts; then mix well.

Peel the bananas, cut into chunks and place on 4 squares of buttered foil. Spoon over the apricot mixture and fold each one up to make a parcel. Put the parcels into a basket in the steamer and cook for 10–15 minutes, depending upon the ripeness of the bananas.

Serve hot, with vanilla ice cream.

Crème Caramels

SERVES 6

Crème Caramels make an elegant light dessert. They may be made in advance and chilled in the refrigerator so make an ideal dessert to serve for a dinner party.

CARAMEL
125 g (4 oz)
  granulated sugar
5 tablespoons cold
  and 1 tablespoon
  hot water
CRÈME
600 ml (1 pint) milk
100 g (3½ oz) sugar
1 teaspoon vanilla
  essence
2 eggs plus 2 egg yolks
butter for greasing

❶ To make the caramel, put the sugar and the cold water into a small heavy saucepan and place over a low heat, stirring until the sugar dissolves. Turn up the heat and boil the syrup for about 10 minutes until it turns a deep golden brown. Take the pan off the heat and add the tablespoon of hot water. Quickly pour the syrup into 6 ramekin dishes.

Pour the milk into another pan and heat until almost boiling. Meanwhile beat the sugar, vanilla essence, eggs and yolks together. Pour the milk on to the egg mixture and whisk until thoroughly blended. Strain into a jug and

DESSERTS AND CAKES

spoon off any froth which rises to the surface. Pour the crème into the ramekin dishes and place in a basket in the steamer. Cover with a piece of buttered greaseproof paper and cook for 25 minutes or until set.

Remove the dishes from the steamer and allow to cool. Refrigerate until required. To serve, run a knife around the edge of the ramekins and reverse each on to a serving plate.

Cabinet Pudding
SERVES 4–6

There are many different ways to make this pudding; this recipe is very easy to prepare.

6 trifle sponges
50 g (2 oz) glacé
   cherries, chopped
25 g (1 oz) caster
   sugar
2 eggs
600 ml (1 pint) milk
1 teaspoon vanilla
   essence
a knob of butter for
   greasing

❶ Cut each sponge into 6 cubes. Place the cubes in a large bowl with the cherries and sugar and toss together.

Beat the eggs, milk and vanilla essence together; then stir into the cake mixture. Leave to stand for 30 minutes.

Butter the inside of a 900 ml (1½-pint) pudding basin and then turn the mixture into it, covering securely with buttered greaseproof paper or foil.

Place in a basket and steam for 45 minutes; then allow to stand in the steamer for a further 15 minutes.

Carefully turn out on to a warmed serving plate.

83

Pears Belle Hélène
SERVES 6
Steamed pears with chocolate sauce are a family favourite.

1 vanilla pod
6 firm pears
SAUCE
175 g (6 oz) plain
    chocolate
200 ml (7 fl oz)
    water
75 g (3 oz)
    granulated sugar

❶ Add the vanilla pod to the reservoir. Peel the pears and core them from the base, leaving the stalks intact. Put the pears in a basket and cook for 25–30 minutes, until they are tender.

Meanwhile, prepare the sauce by putting the chocolate and water in a saucepan and heating gently until melted. Add the sugar and simmer until the sauce becomes smooth and coats the back of a spoon.

Transfer the pears to a serving dish and spoon the chocolate sauce over each.

Peaches Supreme
SERVES 4
A classic dessert, this has a wonderful summer flavour, so do try it when the fruit is in season.

125 g (4 oz) sugar
300 ml (½ pint)
    water
1 vanilla pod
4 large peaches
2 tablespoons flaked
    almonds, toasted
SAUCE
250 g (8 oz)
    strawberries
juice of ½ lemon
50 g (2 oz) icing sugar
1 tablespoon kirsch

❷ Put the sugar, water and vanilla pod into the non-perforated tray and place in the steamer for 10 minutes until the sugar has dissolved. Add the peaches to the syrup and steam for 10–15 minutes, until they are just tender.

Lift the peaches into a bowl and pour over the syrup, discarding the vanilla pod. When cool, remove the skins from the peaches; then leave them to chill in the syrup for at least 1 hour.

To make the sauce, purée the strawberries by rubbing through a sieve, and whisk in the lemon juice, icing sugar and kirsch.

To serve, lift the peaches out of the syrup, and transfer to serving dishes; pour over the sauce and scatter over the almonds.

Pears Belle Hélène
Peaches Supreme

Cherry Cushions
MAKES 8–10
To vary these scone-like desserts, try other flavours of fruit pie filling.

250 g (8 oz) self-
  raising flour, plus
  extra for kneading
75 g (3 oz) butter,
  plus extra for
  greasing
50 g (2 oz) soft light
  brown sugar
1/2 teaspoon ground
  cinnamon
1 egg yolk
milk to mix
1/2 × 400 g (14 oz)
  can of cherry pie
  filling

❷ Put the flour into a bowl with the butter and rub together until the mixture resembles fine breadcrumbs. Stir in the sugar and cinnamon; then add the egg yolk and enough milk to form a soft, but not a sticky, dough. Knead lightly on a floured surface; then roll out to a 5 mm (1/4 inch) thickness.

Using an 8.5 cm (3 1/2-inch) cutter, cut out about 20 rounds. Place a teaspoonful of pie filling on one half of the rounds and dampen the edges. Place the other rounds on top and press the edges together to seal. Put the cushions into lightly greased baskets and cook for 15 minutes.

Serve warm, with whipped cream or greek yogurt.

Blackberry and Apple Winter Puddings
SERVES 4
A warm version of summer pudding. If blackberries are unavailable try plums or lightly cooked rhubarb for a change.

50 g (2 oz) butter,
  melted
soft light brown sugar
  for coating
8–10 thin slices of
  bread, crusts
  removed

FILLING
250 g (8 oz)
  blackberries,
  thawed if frozen

❶ Grease the insides of 4 teacups with some of the butter, and then coat with sugar. Cut the slices of bread in half and use to line the bottom and sides of the cups, reserving a few for the tops. Brush the bread with the rest of the butter.

Put the fruit into a bowl and toss with the cornflour. Stir in the sugar and lemon rind, and then spoon into the bread-lined cups, pressing the filling down with the back of the spoon. Cover with the remaining bread. Place

*1 medium-size
cooking apple,
peeled, cored and
chopped
1 tablespoon cornflour
2 tablespoons soft
light brown sugar
grated rind of
½ lemon*

in a basket in the steamer, cover the cups with a piece of greaseproof paper, and steam for 45 minutes.

To serve, turn out on to plates and serve with thick yogurt or cream.

Jam Sponge Pudding
SERVES 4–6
A family favourite, this recipe can be varied using any flavour jam, or try golden syrup for a change.

*4 tablespoons jam
125 g (4 oz) butter or
margarine, plus
extra for greasing
125 g (4 oz) caster
sugar
2 eggs, beaten
a few drops of vanilla
essence
125 g (4 oz) self-
raising flour,
sieved
1 tablespoon milk*

1½ Grease a 900 ml (1½-pint) pudding basin and spoon the jam into the bottom.

Put the butter or margarine into a bowl with the sugar and beat together until light and creamy. Beat in the eggs, one at a time, and then add the vanilla essence. Fold in the flour and milk and then spoon into the pudding basin. Cover with a pleated piece of buttered greaseproof paper or foil and secure with string. Place in a basket and cook for 1–1¼ hours, or until firm.

Clockwise from top:
Jam Sponge Pudding
Blackberry and Apple
Winter Puddings
Cherry Cushions

Christmas Pudding
SERVES 12–16

125 g (4 oz) self-raising flour
1 teaspoon mixed spice
1 teaspoon ground cinnamon
1 teaspoon grated nutmeg
125 g (4 oz) shredded suet
125 g (4 oz) soft light brown sugar
50 g (2 oz) ground almonds
500 g (1 lb) dried fruit
2 apples, peeled, cored and chopped finely
3 eggs
1 tablespoon black treacle
4 tablespoons milk
butter for greasing

1–2 Sieve the flour and spices into a large mixing bowl; add the suet, sugar, ground almonds and fruit and mix well. Add the eggs and treacle and enough of the milk to form a moist but not wet consistency. Divide the mixture between 2 well buttered 900 ml (1½-pint) pudding basins. Cover each one with a pleated sheet of buttered greaseproof paper or foil and secure with string.

Place the bowls in baskets in the steamer and cook for about 4 hours. Refill the water reservoir as required during the cooking period. When cooked, remove from the steamer and allow to cool. Cover with fresh greaseproof paper and store in a dry airy place until Christmas.

On Christmas day cover again and steam for 1–1½ hours. Serve with brandy butter or whipped cream.

Apple and Vermicelli Pudding
SERVES 6–8
An unusual combination of ingredients, this filling pudding can be enjoyed at any time – serve either hot or at room temperature.

a knob of butter for greasing
a pinch of salt
175 g (6 oz) egg vermicelli

1 Grease a 20 cm (8-inch) soufflé dish with the knob of butter. Bring a pan of salted water to the boil and add the vermicelli, cooking for 3–4 minutes until just *al dente*. Drain, rinse in cold water, and drain again.

2 eggs
3 tablespoons clear
  honey
2 large cooking apples,
  peeled and grated
2 tablespoons lemon
  juice
50 g (2 oz) raisins
50 g (2 oz) walnuts,
  chopped
½ teaspoon mixed
  spice
a pinch of ground
  cloves
50 g (2 oz) butter,
  melted
chopped nuts or icing
  sugar, to serve

In a large bowl beat the eggs with the honey. Add the apples and lemon juice and fold together. Stir in the raisins, walnuts and spices. Then carefully mix in the vermicelli.

Turn the mixture into the dish and pour over the melted butter. Cover with foil, place in a basket and steam for 1 hour.

Serve hot, sprinkled with chopped nuts, or serve at room temperature, dusted with icing sugar.

Chocolate Castle Puddings

MAKES 4–6

Children will love these little puddings, which can be served with custard.

75 g (3 oz) plain
  chocolate
150 ml (¼ pint) milk
150 g (5 oz) sponge
  cake, crumbed
50 g (2 oz) butter,
  plus extra for
  greasing
50 g (2 oz) caster
  sugar
2 eggs, separated
2 drops of vanilla
  essence

❶ Grease small pudding basins or dariole moulds.

Put the chocolate into a saucepan with the milk and heat gently until melted. Stir to blend and then bring to the boil. Pour over the cake crumbs and leave to stand for 25 minutes.

Put the butter and sugar into a bowl and beat until light and fluffy. Beat in the egg yolks and then add the cake crumb mixture and vanilla essence. Whisk the egg whites until stiff and fold into the mixture. Divide between the basins and place in baskets in the steamer. Cover with a piece of greased greaseproof paper and cook for 15–20 minutes or until set.

Apricot Upside-down Pudding

SERVES 6–8

A delicious variation of a family favourite; use wholemeal bread and flour for a nuttier flavour and texture.

25 g (1 oz) butter,
plus extra for
greasing
175 g (6 oz) soft light
brown sugar
400 g (14 oz) can of
apricot halves,
drained
125 g (4 oz) sunflower
margarine
2 eggs, beaten
75 g (3 oz) semi-dried
apricots, chopped
50 g (2 oz) pecans or
walnuts, chopped
50 g (2 oz) fresh
breadcrumbs
125 g (4 oz) self-
raising flour
½ teaspoon ground
cinnamon
1 teaspoon baking
powder

❶ Grease the sides of a 20 cm (8-inch) round soufflé dish.

Melt the butter in a saucepan, stir in 50 g (2 oz) of the sugar and then spread the mixture over the base of the dish. Arrange the apricot halves on top of this mixture.

In a bowl beat the remaining sugar and the margarine together until creamy, and then gradually beat in the eggs. Stir in the chopped apricots and nuts. Mix the breadcrumbs, flour, cinnamon and baking powder together and fold into the mixture. Spoon this on top of the apricot halves and level the surface.

Cover the pudding with a piece of greased greaseproof paper, place in a basket and steam for 45 minutes. Remove from the steamer and run a knife around the edge of the pudding. Turn on to a warm serving plate and serve with cream or custard.

*Apricot Upside-down
Pudding
Chocolate Castle
Puddings*

Hazelnut and Banana Tea Loaf

SERVES 6–8

**This loaf is better made a day or two in advance to allow the flavour to mature.
Serve sliced and buttered.**

125 g (4 oz) butter,
   plus extra for
   greasing
175 g (6 oz) soft light
   brown sugar
2 eggs, beaten
250 g (8 oz) self-
   raising flour
1 teaspoon baking
   powder
2–3 tablespoons milk
50 g (2 oz) hazelnuts,
   chopped and
   toasted lightly
2 ripe bananas
2 teaspoons lemon
   juice
icing sugar to dredge

Grease and line a 1 kg (2 lb) loaf tin.
   Put the butter, sugar, eggs, flour, baking powder and milk into a food processor and process until well blended. Add the hazelnuts and work again to mix in.
   Mash the bananas with the lemon juice on a plate and then add to the cake mix and blend in. Spoon the mixture into the prepared tin and level smooth.
   Place in a basket in the steamer and cook for 60–70 minutes until the loaf is well risen and firm to touch. Turn out on to a wire rack to cool; then dredge with icing sugar.

Lightning Cake

MAKES A 500 g (1 lb) LOAF

Use a good quality cake mix of any flavour to make a loaf cake when in a hurry.

Make up the cake mix as directed on the packet. Turn the mixture into a 500 g (1 lb) foil loaf tin, place in a basket and steam for 20 minutes or until risen and firm.
   Allow to cool and then decorate with butter icing or glacé icing and nuts, if wished.

INDEX